Animal Helpers: Aquariums

by Jennifer Keats Curtis
with The Florida Aquarium,
Georgia Aquarium, Monterey
Bay Aquarium, National
Aquarium, Shedd Aquarium,
and Tennessee Aquarium

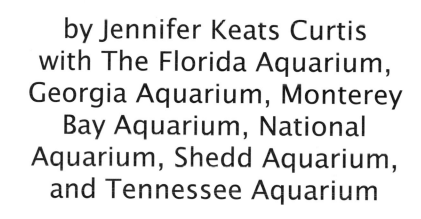

You won't need a snorkel and mask in here! In an aquarium, you can trek through millions of gallons of fresh and salt water, but you won't get wet.

Walk, rather than swim, by amazing aquatic creatures in tanks and exhibits. Visit animals born at the aquarium, like this penguin chick and little fish.

Gentoo penguin

sailfin sculpin

sea otters

sea lion

See mammals like these sea otters and this sea lion. Learn about reptiles like this sea turtle, who was rescued in the wild.

loggerhead sea turtle

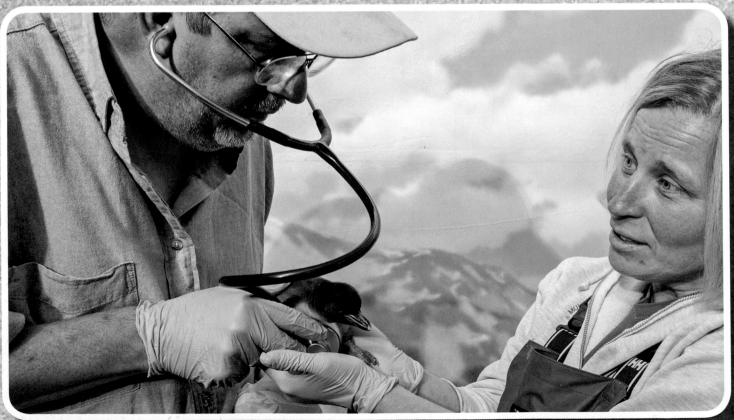

Lots of people work in aquariums, such as aquarists, biologists, curators, and volunteers. They care for creatures found all over the world, from those that swim near the tops of lakes to those that dive into the ocean's depths.

weedy sea dragon

At the aquarium, you can get a close-up look at animals and underwater plants. Some of these you may have only read about or heard of, like this exotic seahorse and these jellyfish.

Indonesian jellyfish

Aquariums hold saltwater and freshwater animals. This hammerhead shark, tiny octopus, and enormous manta ray come from the salty ocean.

scalloped hammerhead

red octopus

manta ray

pike

white sucker

pumpkinseed
sunfish

These fishes come from
freshwater rivers and lakes.

walleye

ocean
sunfish

In an aquarium, you can see huge, finned fish and very tiny fish.

shortsnout
seahorses

You can find cold-weather animals and warm-water fish.

Gentoo penguins

African black-footed penguins

Mandarinfish

Garibaldi

Would *you* like to work in an aquarium?

Could you transport whale sharks, work in a water quality lab, or feed sea otters?

sea otters

Would you like to teach a sea lion? Could you train river otters and dolphins?

sea lion

river otter

Atlantic bottlenose dolphins

river otter

If you worked in an aquarium, you might save an otter, treat a sick electric eel, or listen to a newborn penguin's heartbeat.

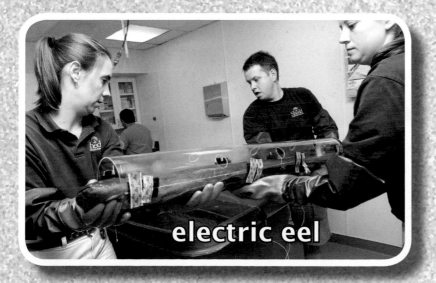

electric eel

macaroni penguin

Could you release a cured sea turtle back into the ocean? Would you research sharks and help alligators?

Kemp's ridley sea turtle

sevengill
shark

albino American alligator

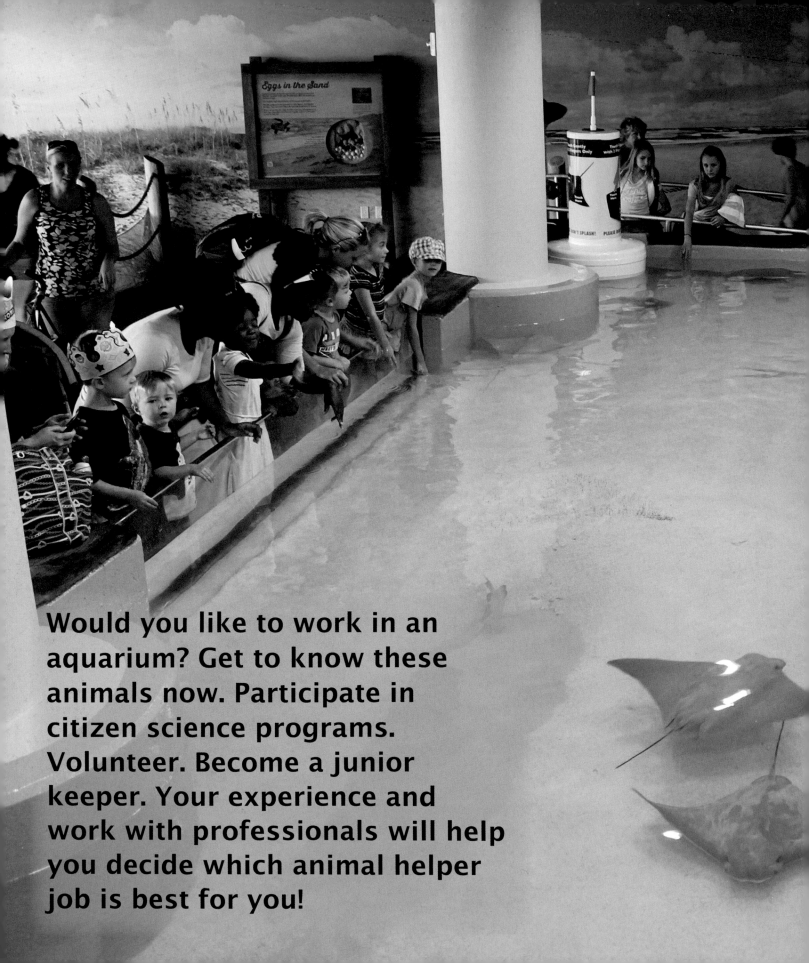

Would you like to work in an aquarium? Get to know these animals now. Participate in citizen science programs. Volunteer. Become a junior keeper. Your experience and work with professionals will help you decide which animal helper job is best for you!

For Creative Minds

Aquarium Jobs

There are many jobs in an aquarium! An aquarium needs lots of different experts and volunteers.

Experts who feed, clean, and care for aquatic animals that live in tanks are called **aquarists**.

Aquariums are not just for animals that live in the water! Many aquariums have an aviary, a place that houses birds. The experts who care for these birds are **aviculturists**.

Biologists study all kinds of living beings. They examine how living things grow, reproduce, and relate to their environment. There are many different kinds of specialties in biology. A biologist who studies reptiles and amphibians is a **herpetologist**. A biologist who studies fish is an **ichthyologist**.

A person who manages the exhibits is a **curator**. Curators create spaces where people can learn about and connect with the creatures in the aquarium.

Animals get sick sometimes and need a doctor. **Veterinarians** are medical doctors who take care of animals.

Aquariums often have lots of **volunteers**. People do not have to be scientists to volunteer at an aquarium. But for people who do want to become scientists or work at an aquarium, volunteering is a great place to start! Volunteers greet and educate guests, prepare food and feed the animals. They also help maintain the tanks and sometimes even dive in the tanks to feed the fish or assist with cleaning.

Match the Animal

1. This endangered **bird** cannot fly in the air. Instead, it dives, swims, and waddles to get around. Chicks are covered in gray fluff that turns into sleek, black-and-white feathers by adulthood. This bird is named for the continent on which it is found.

2. These playful and intelligent **mammals** have four flipper feet that allow them to move easily in the water and on land. They live mostly along the Pacific coast from southern Canada all the way to Mexico. A separate group lives in the Galapagos Islands. These animals live in large groups and rest by making a raft where they gather together and float on their backs.

3. This giant **mollusk** has eight legs and a lifespan of only 3 to 5 years. It is one of the most intelligent species of animals in the world and its brain is the largest of all invertebrates (animals without a backbone or spinal cord). It lives in the coastal waters of the northern Pacific Ocean and grows to about 16 feet (5m) in length.

4. This **reptile** has a hard shell and can weigh up to 100 pounds (45kg). It lives near the coast in the western Atlantic Ocean and the Gulf of Mexico. Due to pollution and hunting, this animal is critically endangered.

5. This giant animal is the world's largest **fish**. It lives in tropical and temperate water all around the world. It is a filter-feeder that eats mostly plankton. This fish is a slow mover and swims about as fast as a human walks—roughly 3 miles (5km) per hour!

A. Giant Pacific Octopus

B. Whale shark

C. African penguin, also called black-footed penguin

D. Kemp's ridley sea turtle

E. California sea lion

Answers: 1-C, 2-E, 3-A, 4-D, 5-B

True or False

1. Aquariums work to conserve and protect species that are at risk or endangered.

2. Dolphins and whales are a type of fish.

3. There are many different jobs in an aquarium.

4. The blue whale is the world's largest fish.

5. Beluga whales are one of the smallest species of whale in the world.

6. All sharks live in salt water.

7. The fastest fish in the world can swim nearly as fast as a cheetah can run.

8. Ocean sunfish can lay more than three million eggs each spawning season.

9. In order to volunteer at an aquarium, you need a college degree in science.

10. All aquarium animals live in water.

Answers: 1-True. 2-False: Dolphins and whales breathe air and are mammals, not fish. 3-True. 4-False: The blue whale is a mammal, not a fish. The largest fish in the world is the whale shark. The biggest whale shark ever measured was 40 feet (12.2 meters) long. 5-True. 6-False. Most sharks live in salty oceans and seas, but there are five freshwater shark species in Southeast Asia and Australia. 7-True. The Atlantic sailfish can reach speeds of 70 miles (110km) per hour. 8-True. 9-False. 10-False. Aquariums also keep birds, snakes, and animals from many different habitats all around the world.

Animal Fun Facts

Beluga whales live in the arctic and subarctic in groups called pods. When born, belugas are dark grey. As they get older, their color lightens. By the time they are adults, they are completely white.

Sea otters have the thickest fur of all animals. Their dense fur coat keeps them warm even in icy water. Sea otters are endangered and live in the northern Pacific Ocean.

Manta rays are the biggest of all rays. They can weigh as much as 3,000 pounds (1360 kg) and have up to a 29 foot (9 meter) wingspan. Mantas live alone and swim in tropical seas and oceans around the world.

Moray eels live around the world in tropical and temperate waters. They are shy animals and hide in rocky crevices and reefs. Morays hide in rocks and wait for their prey to come near enough for them to grab.

American alligators are native to the southeastern United States. Albino alligators are very rare and are known as "ghosts of the swamp." Albino American alligators cannot survive in the wild because they are very sensitive to direct sunlight.

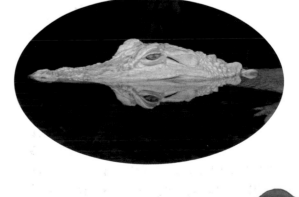

For my nephew and niece, Braden and Finley Keats, who share my love and compassion for all creatures, great and small.—JKC

Thanks to the following aquariums for their photographs and knowledge:
° The Florida Aquarium, www.flaquarium.org
° Georgia Aquarium, www.georgiaaquarium.org
° Monterey Bay Aquarium, www.montereybayaquarium.org
° National Aquarium, www.aqua.org
° Shedd Aquarium, www.sheddaquarium.org
° Tennessee Aquarium, www.tnaqua.org

Library of Congress Cataloging-in-Publication Data

Curtis, Jennifer Keats, author.
  Aquariums / by Jennifer Keats Curtis with The Florida Aquarium, Georgia Aquarium, Monterey Bay Aquarium, National Aquarium, Shedd Aquarium, and Tennessee Aquarium.
      pages cm. -- (Animal helpers)
  Audience: 4-9.
   ISBN 978-1-62855-203-4 (English hardcover) -- ISBN 978-1-62855-212-6 (English pbk.) -- ISBN 978-1-62855-221-8 (Spanish pbk.) -- ISBN 978-1-62855-230-0 (English ebook downloadable) -- ISBN 978-1-62855-239-3 (Spanish ebook downloadable) -- ISBN 978-1-62855-248-5 (English ebook dual language enhanced) -- ISBN 978-1-62855-257-7 (Spanish ebook dual language enhanced) 1. Public aquariums--Employees--Juvenile literature. 2. Public aquariums--Juvenile literature. 3. Aquarium animals--Juvenile literature. I. Title. II. Series: Curtis, Jennifer Keats. Animal helpers.
  QL78.C85 2014
  639.34'4--dc23
                            2013044815

Photo credits:

The Florida Aquarium: aquarium workers, Kemp's ridley sea turtle, river otter, stingrays
Georgia Aquarium: African penguin, albino American alligator, beluga whale, manta ray, sea otter, water
    quality lab, weedy sea dragons, whale shark
Monterey Bay Aquarium: aquarium workers, blackfooted (African) penguin, Garibaldi, Indonesian jellyfish,
    loggerhead sea turtle, Mandarinfish, ocean sunfish, red octopus, sailfin sculpin, scalloped hammerhead, sea
    otter, sevengill shark, shortsnout seahorses, white sturgeon
National Aquarium: aquarium, aquarium workers, Atlantic bottlenose dolphins, coral reef, giant Pacific
    octopus, moray eel, two-toed sloth
Shedd Aquarium: aquarium workers, California sea lion, electric eel, pike, pumpkinseed sunfish, walleye,
    white sucker
Tennessee Aquarium: aquarium workers, Gentoo penguin, river otter, stingrays

Also available in Spanish as *Ayudantes de animales: acuarios*.

Lexile® Level: 910
key phrases for educators: EE (Environmental Education), human interaction, life science, threatened/
endangered, water habitats (ocean, lakes, ponds, wetlands, rivers),

Manufactured in China, December 2013
This product conforms to CPSIA 2008
First Printing

Sylvan Dell Publishing
Mt. Pleasant, SC 29464
www.SylvanDellPublishing.com